My husband
is learning to draw.

poems by

Mamie Morgan

Finishing Line Press
Georgetown, Kentucky

My husband
is learning to draw.

ACKNOWLEDGMENTS

Much love to Alan, the husband in question. While I wish your childhood had been filled with more art, more gentleness, less of everything else—witnessing you make up for lost time continues to restore my faith in magic. Hell, it pretty much restores my faith in everything.

"My husband is learning to draw a leather jacket" and "My husband names the field he's drawing femur" first appeared on terrain.org. "My husband can't stop talking about the sex lives of anglerfish" was originally published in sixth finch.

Publisher: Leah Huete de Maines
Editor: Christen Kincaid
Cover Art and Design: Hannah Hunt and Alan Hester
Author Photo: Julia Sears

Order online: www.finishinglinepress.com
also available on amazon.com

Author inquiries and mail orders:
Finishing Line Press
PO Box 1626
Georgetown, Kentucky 40324
USA

Contents

for Alan

Last summer, two discrete young snakes left their skin
on my small porch, two mornings in a row. Being

postmodern now, I pretended as if I did not see
them, nor understand what I knew to be circling

inside me.

—Robin Coste Lewis

I was thinkin' about who you are.

—Harry Styles

My husband is learning to draw a leather jacket

from an expat on YouTube
living in Yokohama with her family.
He copies Van Gogh's wheat stacks, his chickens,

pens single words suspended in the mid-air of printer paper,
then scrawls angry cumulous clouds overtop to make them disappear.

I like to imagine what they might have been:
engine, sanctuary, dazzling reinforcement. He never draws
bombs or helicopters, severed limbs or faces, so when he makes me

into a picture I'm looking away toward a mosaic of lakes, holding my dead
father's hand. He draws proverbs, eyeglasses, the train station and two beers

from that Hemingway story. When we fly,
we tuck my husband's hands into the seatbelt so
he doesn't accidentally punch a passenger in his sleep.

My husband will do anything to leave the world and anything
to remain inside of it. Just last week our neighbor meant to drive

his wife to Thursday's Bingo at church but
something in his brain went wonks and they ended up
in an Orlando CVS parking lot, my sister's favorite city from

this world. My husband is ashamed of his penmanship so sometimes
I find him writing What on earth is going on? in cursive, over and over.

I don't like to imagine the pamphlet
of soldiers who take pleasure in war, though
we know they exist. What my sister loves about Orlando

is her one week in it years ago time-buoyed on a hammock,
the hotel pool water dyed gem-mine purple. So much sand trafficked

in that no sadness could infiltrate her.
I never asked our dad if he missed being able to walk,

and when my husband draws bridges, they're built of small crosshatching strikes.
When I ask where they're headed he says *nowhere* like it's obvious,

kind of beaming.

My husband discovers Janis Joplin well into the pandemic

and he's most concerned about the health of her hair,
what argon oil deep conditioning treatment

she might could use some fifty years after her death.
For a literature teacher, I learned the term *penultimate*

embarrassingly late, like the summer that was all Lizzo
lawn seats and Rapinoe swinging in gold, fists

to the sun like some best kind of hazard, while
we cheered from a crap bar in Oregon

called BAR. My husband grew up on WHAM!
and tanning beds in which he wore nothing

but a sock to cover his junk and boys who stole
his sneaks after so much time on layaway,

on Holiday Inn antics where he worked housekeeping
between weekends serving Guard. Our third date

he leaned up to flip the light switch and I spotted
this tummy tattoo of a banana pepper

laughing in a top hat someone needled into him
as a child. Half lasered off, half stubborn-grinning

like my old friend Chris Sterling from grade school
who last I saw was doped up and spinning out

in his jammies, trying to convince us he was okay but
also that his two thumbs had become spaceships,

he was trying so hard to land them inside his pockets,
trying so hard to warn us of all the bad shit fixing to happen.

An hour before the man I'm waiting on at table 200 goes into cardiac arrest, he asks for a stack of cocktail napkins,

draws on each of them fully-formed ships,
like from inside a bottle or old movie. When my husband

sketches a parrot he enjoys the beginning most, before their feathers
have even happened. In October I take off work so I can work
with middle schoolers

along the Ohio West Virginia line. We play imaginary
show and tell even though they're too old: Candace wants to bring

her goat, Cole wishes we could all see his dead grandfather's spoon collection,
every spot on each one of his cows. If Hunter could go anywhere
in the world, it would be

Blake Shelton's restaurant 360 miles east of here.
I'm a little hungover and trying to teach them something

about image or life and Candace won't shut up about the goat: *We keep it
tied to my uncle's Chevy Impala outside our trailer but don't be sad, the lead*

is long and she can go just about anywhere she wants. In the closet
of my childhood bedroom my mother finds a three-ring binder filled with poems

I wrote twenty years ago. On the cover, inexplicably: a photograph
of Audrey Hepburn

kicking up her certain heels. I read a few of them with one eye open to the truth
that my crutch

has always been specificity, upholstery over stuffing. If the poem's about
Chad Hammett fucking with me in carpool, I want to include the make and

model of every bumper sticker. Like this morning, a bunch of young people,
windows down, blaring Aretha Franklin's *Think* at the intersection of Poinsett

and Pleasantburg, just a few shy blocks from where two cops
are hurling a child protestor into space. No one cares what color the car is,

the vessels of transport poems can sometimes keep perfectly still.
Heading back to my Ohio-side motel, I saw Candace's goat,
knew her by the Impala

and the lead and the way her hooves tap-danced against the engine

                    like some kind of knocking inside my brain.

My husband names the field he's drawing Femur,

titles the graphite rock souffle
over which a pilot flies Doorway, names
the first turkey he ever sketches *War*, confessing

that plumage is the ultimate motherfucker for his shaking hands.
He's distrustful of windchimes, boys rough-housing in the street before dark,

enjoys those pale ales that don't
have any booze in them. Any school stuff
he's learned comes from library books so there exists

a zillion words he's never heard aloud: crevasse, *Bronte, glissando,*
jubilance. He's flown over Wichita, Kabul, Bucharest, the back of a bull

before he turned twelve for money.
When we met, my husband slept on a mat and stored
barrels of salt beneath the floorboards of his own home. To cure

meat, to fallow thy neighbor's land if pressed. All kid-me knew to threaten
at the dead end of Lawson's Fork Creek after anyone tried to pull down my shorts

or drew a pen knife or claimed to know
the Buick tag numbers of my gramma was:
I'm going home, as if that amounted to anything more

than a place we passed on the way to some private sector of woods
that actually listened the few times we cropped up crying. My husband's

painting of a moat places second
at Fayetteville's county fair. He's unhappy
with the crowds, not the pastel of two lambs

hunkered down in a Wal-Mart parking lot taking gold.
My husband's never heard the word *satire*, doesn't think there's anything

funny about getting lost.

Rijksmuseum, and a woman in periwinkle wants her boyfriend to photograph her ascending:

Make sure my hair is right, and she's got a good point,
it's fabulous, all ringlets like a kid's before we're taught

to tamp down whatever's wild like this single file line
of elementary students marching into the sixteenth century

bedecked in matching white lab coats. My husband wonders
what a childhood with art in it might be like. He loves

Still Life with Gilt Cup, all her varying pewters, her
spiraling rind. The French possess that phrase, to deceive

the eye, *trompe l'oeil*, like the middle aged man I dated
who every other weekend snuck up to a sophomore

in Knoxville named Alex, University of Tennessee, Go Vols.
Had work in Darlington is what he said, detailed the racetrack,

the sound a rare rain made against the tin roof of his Airbnb,
what brand of beer he drank with this old guy next door. I find

the excellently haired woman staring into a still life with shells,
ocean-spirals like the head of a Smith and Wesson tactical pen

my husband's brought abroad for the summer. He can't imagine
being disarmed, and I hate every war every government's sent

anyone to. In training, they made him white out all the places
his name might exist, from trunk to uniform. *What did they call you,*

I ask. *Number 206*, he's rubbing graphite into the rough draft
of a lone cypress. My husband enjoys the akimbo vantage point

of any one thing at a time he's making: a single building,
a friendship, a single lemon rind rogue-tunneling out of its clothes.

Ashley's having trouble killing people

in this early draft, her first thriller—
a terrarium of grown sisters pocked along
the Pontchartrain. Maybe one of them

should marry? Maybe one should recede
into the creaking corners of a secret life?
It's the 1960's. Ashley isn't even born yet,

doesn't know who will become the murderer,
some surprise brother we discover way late
or what. Her last novel studied a chef who

ends up settling in California with a secret child.
I couldn't tell if you were supposed to be sad
at the end or what. Maybe a decade before Ash

would tell me anything about anything.
In high school the old guy I dated took us
to Orlando for a rave. He drove a semi

and could pop his armory of teeth in and out.
The club reached four stories, a different theme
on every floor. I remember hauling ass

through the jungle, up the stairs into eighties prom.
It felt like the kind of running a movie girl does
just before she's stabbed. He found me

on the roof, open-aired and themeless,
my heels against the edge, where I wanted
to leave him for anyone. Ashley's thinking yes,

nuptials, clues hidden inside each gift.
Everyone loves a wedding. Everyone loves
to figure out the ending, finally, and weep into it.

It's spring, and my husband thinks Josh Groban wrote Hallelujah,

rubs lichen from a flower arrangement into his drawing of a fish owl,
dips Q-tips into espresso to fill out its chest feathers. Instead of telling him

about the worst days of my life, I list every fabulous moniker
from this morning's visit to the vet: Techno, Sonja Morgan, Alma Mater,

some beagle puppy called Grief. A woman in limestone scrubs says:
After my wife left, I renamed our housecat Eris, goddess of chaos.

In the miniseries we watch, they're pinning this woman's murder
on a husband or a hawk. I'm always gunning for any animal

whose flaws I put all inklings of faith inside. When she wants to bite,
our pit bull corrects her mouth into a lick, some whole narrative

in under a beat, bait dog from Nicholtown before we found her
on Instagram wearing a cobalt chevroned sweater. When we first

moved in together, my husband and I nailed a sage green mailbox
to our kitchen wall, where we placed all the things we couldn't bear

to say out loud:

> *I'm afraid of my own debts, I still sleep*
> *with a stuffed duck named Slipper, no one has ever stayed.*

Five years old, running through a London park filled with gnomes.
Nearby, the smell of burned-up bread. Our mom let me buy a postcard

of river-swimming deer from a museum shop I kept folded four ways
in my pocket, addressed to our home, confidante and protectress.

I didn't know what three wishes to ask of it, only that the sky rustled and
dusk'd come on and to survive I'd need every dog I'd ever bet on to win.

When M'Randa drives grocery delivery with the baby strapped to her and the rich folks don't tip

we google the tax history
of their homes, find their LinkedIn
profiles, make the rest up over a bottle
of Lidl rosé I bring to her house. One couple
owns a whole school, Christian, K-8. One lady makes

M'Randa carry six hundred dollars
worth of goods up three flights of stairs,
yells at her on the landing over the price of
Boar's Head ham. I never know how to stick up
for anybody, even kids at whom my boss yelled when I taught

high school. This morning,
everyone's telling Amy Ziegler Happy Birthday!
on their stories. When we were little her father owned
the town toy store and sometimes people made fun of her
for being loud or Jewish or both. When Johnny Kramer stabbed her lip

with a stick on the trampoline
I punched him square in the dick.
Whole walk home he yelled how he'd
be back, a threat that rang in our ears for a while
before fading into the untrimmed magnolia of someone's

vacant lot. I want to say Happy Birthday!
as well but when I get to Amy's Instagram she's dead.
She's been dead. Her last picture was forever ago, Thanksgiving
with her family when her hair began growing back. She's dyed it hazard
pink and is laughing. In high school after a night of partying Amy stared into

the bathroom mirror and said, *We look like*
something they put out to scare the crows. You can't
expect people to make any kind of sense. My old boss
is a vegetarian but shoots squirrels in his backyard and reads
Eat, Pray, Love for fun. He used to say things like, *What the fuck*

is wrong with you? He used to write me into
his stories as the village slut. But whatever. I also kind of
loved him. This one time M'Randa scaled the fence of her neighbor,
stole the cattle dog they left out to freeze, wrapped him in a towel—broken
pink umbrellas on one side, peach seagulls pumping heavenward on the other.

The Lady of Shalott is taking a breather

in storage after so much time on loan, all that
polite bustle, who can blame her, but it isn't the same,
talking shit about the women in Rutherston's Laundry Girls

who aren't laundry girls at all but models who sell fine fruit from a stall.
Earlier, on the balcony, wearing only my husband's flak jacket, I wanted him

to want to take my photograph—
it would've been a good one—then felt dumb about it.
At the war museum, a boy wishing out of the Wurzburg exhibit

and a father saying no, not until you hear the story of the man you're named for.
Reconciling all this trouble sends me to a bathroom stall between
    Kosovo and Cyprus

where the kid's wailing never seems to dim.
This sounds so silly, but I'd thought if my husband
could meet The Lady of Shalott he'd understand something

tired and brazen and very old inside me only a child's brave enough
to describe. I am trying to reconnect a Zara bag filled with silky things,
    half a leopard

print bikini, one mesh top through which you can see
anything, to a woman who left it in the museum café. When

we meet in the cloak room she offers a thank you, says *it's one of those days*
where, as much as I beg, my mind won't just come on and make it work
    inside my body.

A woman who follows me on Instagram messages to say
her pit bull suffocated on an empty bag of potato chips,

she's halfway through warning every dog parent
from the internet she knows. In special forces school

they kept my husband in a box so long
he came out walking on his knees. He's drawing

a bespectacled gray-headed guy who sports green cords,
makes his feet real teeny, names him Ol' Man Wheeler,

says, *he's my new pal.* We eat BBQ at a picnic table
with a Colonel Bruce Hampton portrait painted on it.

My husband wonders what battles he fought
before I have time to explain. I wait weeks to tell

my husband about the potato chips. *Inside,* he correct,
he suffocated inside the bag, not on it, and I don't speak

to him for days. We never know what to protect
each other from. But there's good news, too. Ol' Man

Wheeler gets a cat whose eyes, depending on the light,
become green, become yellow. It's new so they don't know

how to believe in each other just yet. My husband's still
in the planning stages and his soul's all wobbly,

half filled with sand,
            half somehow still filled with delight.

My husband draws a rubber duckie he won at the movies seven different ways

in an attempt to learn value, shading,
how not to lose one's shit on Zoom calls.

He's tried decaf, jiu jitsu, every breathing exercise
the doctor throws at him. Going to the movies helps,

where I spend the entire film not knowing
our lead is Phillip Seymour Hoffman's kid.

One existential tick I've got is googling the age
of anyone we see on screen. Tom Waits is 72,

but by the time anyone reads this he'll be older
or dead. For years we threw a Waits dinner party

on his birthday, December, which is maybe why
the songs always remind me of Christmas

and enormity, leave me crying in cars
that are parked and cars that are going.

My husband would choose T Swift over Waits
any day of the week. He doesn't need

more frozen-leaved darkness. He buys
the birds who eat from our feeder special seed,

studies them for hours in the morning.
He prefers a ten minute version over anything.

When my husband and I pretend to move to London

we worry most about how we'll transport the dogs abroad
since we read once about an airline that accidentally redirected

a German Shepherd to Japan, only for his owner to find out
when the official handed him someone else's Great Dane

on the tarmac of Kansas City International. We're thinking
an imaginary walk-up in Dulwich or Knightsbridge, though

I'd at one time hoped for Notting Hill, long before my husband
confessed that Portobello Road's market reminds him of war.

When we were kids my sister spent the summers prisoning
fireflies into jars so that at bedtime she could release them

into her room. *Who wouldn't want to feel like they're inside
the middle of a Christmas tree?* she'd ask, as they fell.

It's 1999, and my boyfriend's mom wants to know which one I am.

She's pinning clothes to the line, and I'm not surprised
there are others. His vintage white Mustang wears a painted red horse

galloping down the passenger side. His teeth look like Chicklets
under the black light every time we get high, every time

he asks me to leave. But when my family vacations in New Orleans,
I walk all the way to Lakeside Mall so that a woman can spray Cool Water

cologne on both my wrists. I don't just want to smell like him.
I want a wink of sleep where there's no gatekeeper in the gallery

of my dreams, where I don't have to cherish anybody to exist. I want
to tell my kid self that the best part about loving him will be that walk.

My husband can't stop talking about the sex lives of anglerfish

whose scientific detailing he learned during a virtual art class
        on stippling. Entire pictures made from teensy dots, imagine

        the tedium of it, but every day I say a silent prayer of thanks
to anything that has gotten my husband out of bed: our backyard

family of vermilion flycatchers, that Larry McMurtry audiobook,
        thank you 90's hip-hop Spotify playlist, newly discovered edamame

        hummus recipe, the shots he's learned to give himself in the ass,
thank you handle of Benchmark, quality gear shop who carries

the underwear he likes, even if they cost more than my light bill
        each month during college. Just this morning a horse with his empty

        carriage waiting for some tourist to pull made me so sad
I sat down sobbing smack dab in Jackson Square. We all know

Ryan Adams is a dick, but sometimes when I hear that song
        I've got a really good heart, I just can't catch a break the girl

        I used to be busts into a gajillion easy pieces. Everything's so
embarrassing: low-pile carpet, the pills, all those Dr. Phil

workbooks I completed with magenta pen late high school.
        There's one prayer made tiny-quiet in my head that thanks

        my husband for his willingness to return to pleasure, even when
his pain rings like a jazz band of witnesses from a Hollywood court case,

all of whom turn up missing. Thank you to the monocle he learns
        to build just in case we get thrown into the seventeenth century.

        Thank you to the baby goat we saw being pulled down Frenchmen
in a Radio Flyer who wore an edible ivy wreath around her neck.

Thank you, maybe most, to the child wearing Halloween pajamas in July who mid-party screamed into a room full of grown-ups:

Fine. I'll go to bed. But none of you fuckers can ever make me die.

Mamie Morgan's poems and essays have appeared in *Washington Square Review, Muzzle, Smartish Pace, Cimarron, The Greensboro Review, Inkwell, Carolina Quarterly, Oxford American, Four Way Review, Nimrod, Fish Barrel Review, Glass, The Yalobusha Review, Terrain*, and elsewhere. She holds an MFA in Poetry from UNC Wilmington and a BA in English and Religious Studies from Wofford College. Mamie owns an independent bridal shop in South Carolina and waitresses any shift she can get. Her first full-length collection, *Everyone I've Danced With Is Dead*, is forthcoming from JackLeg Press.

www.ingramcontent.com/pod-product-compliance
Lightning Source LLC
Chambersburg PA
CBHW022106080426
42734CB00009B/1499